This book was made possible by a grant from Kungkungan Bay Resort

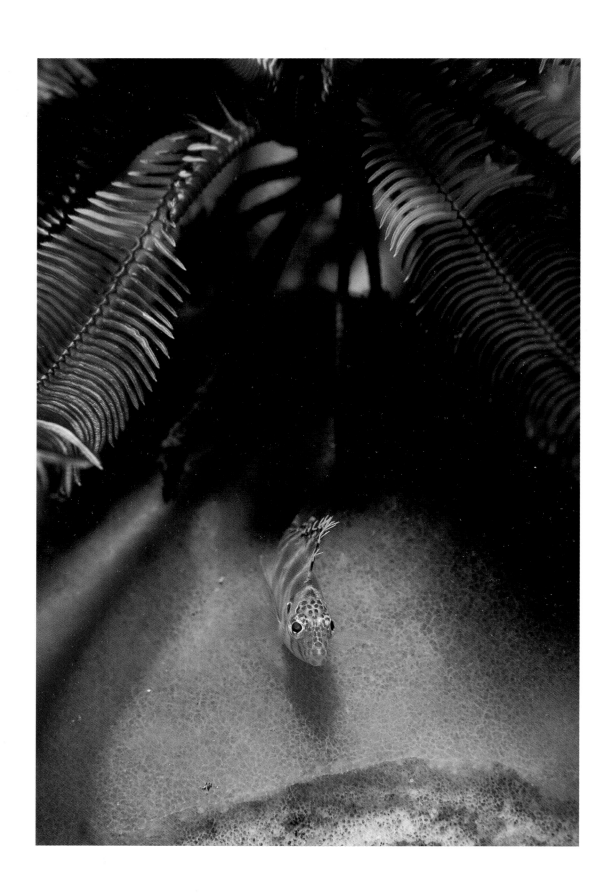

SULAWESI SEAS

INDONESIA'S MAGNIFICENT UNDERWATER REALM

MIKE SEVERNS

TEXT BY MIKE SEVERNS AND PAULINE FIENE-SEVERNS

STAPLES
ECENBARGER
PUBLISHING

THE PUBLISHERS WISH TO THANK THE MAYOR OF BITUNG,

DRS. S.H. SARUNDAJANG, WITHOUT WHOM THIS BOOK

WOULD NOT HAVE BEEN POSSIBLE

PRODUCED AND PUBLISHED BY
STAPLES ECENBARGER PUBLISHING
P.O. BOX 5577
CONCORD, CALIFORNIA 94524
FAX: (510) 825-0105

PHOTO EDITING, DESIGN, EDITING AND CARTOGRAPHY BY DAVID PICKELL

PRODUCTION LIASON: MARY CHIA, PERIPLUS (S) PTE. LTD., SINGAPORE
SET IN TRIPLEX, DRAWN BY ZUZANA LICKO OF EMIGRÉ
COLOR SEPARATIONS BY PICA COLOUR SEPARATION (PTE.) LTD., SINGAPORE
PRINTED AND BOUND BY TIEN WAH PRESS (PTE.) LTD., SINGAPORE

ENDPAPERS: SHALLOW WATER HARD CORALS OFF NORTH SULAWESI

HALF-TITLE: THE COMMON SEA KRAIT, LATICAUDA COLUBRINA

FIRST SPREAD: FISHERMAN OVER THE REEFTOP AT BUNAKEN ISLAND

SECOND SPREAD: TASSLED SCORPIONFISH, SCORPAENOPSIS OXYCEPHALA, AND THE DAMSELFISH CHROMIS VIRIDIS

FRONTISPIECE: A YOUNG BLOTCHED HAWKFISH, CIRRHITICHTHYS APRINUS

TO OUR FRIENDS, RUTH AND ROD DYERLY

WHOSE LOVE OF DIVING STARTED US ON THE ROAD THAT LED TO THIS BOOK

SEAHORSE: HIPPOCAMPUS KUDA

INTRODUCTION

MIKE SEVERNS

Seven years ago, Pauline and I began diving in Indonesia along the coral walls of the islands in the Bunaken Marine Preserve, a few miles offshore from the city of Manado in North Sulawesi. The conditions were nearly perfect. Sunny skies and warm, clear water with magnificent soft corals, giant cuttlefish and clouds of spectacular anthias.

The variety and richness of life was overwhelming, and there seemed to be an endless supply of subjects—I was in photographer's heaven. But after several years of returning to the drop-offs of Bunaken, Manado Tua and the other islands in the preserve, my excitement began to wane. The animals I was seeing were too familiar, and I felt I was no longer breaking new ground.

To find new species and recapture some of that initial excitement, we began to follow the drop-offs deeper, and deeper, and deeper. At one point we were regularly visiting a deep wave bench, a horizontal cleft created by waves pounding against the shoreline ten thousand years ago. An artifact of a time when the sea was considerably shallower than today, this 12-foot-deep and 15-foot-high groove lies 240 feet underwater.

To visit the wave bench is to go back in time, descending along vertical walls that once loomed high above the surface of the sea. Plants clung to cracks in the limestone and the cliffs were crowned by thick forest. Ten thousand years ago, people may have walked where we were diving, and fished along the shoreline defined by this ancient wave bench. Bunaken then was very different from today's beach-ringed island, protected by shallow reef flats.

It was addicting to dive deep and to see animals that live in a world where light is filtered through hundreds of feet of seawater. This great notch cut into Bunaken's cliffs by Pleistocene seas sprouted spectacular sponges and soft corals, and in it lived deep-dwelling fish, foraging in the shadow of the sheer coral wall above.

The danger on these dives came not only from ourselves and our equipment, but from the animals encoun-

AFTER MANY FRUITLESS DAYS DIVING AT SITES UP AND DOWN THE LEMBEH STRAIT LOOKING FOR SEAHORSES, I FOUND THE ONE PICTURED HERE RIGHT IN KUNGKUNGAN BAY, LITERALLY A STONE'S THROW IN FRONT OF THE COTTAGE WHERE WE WERE STAYING.

tered as well. On several occasions, big sharks swam up behind me while I was taking pictures deep on the wall. Usually I would see their reflections in the glass of my camera's viewfinder, then turn to see them leaving. Sometimes we would meet face to face, and in spite of their obvious advantage in size and ability, they would always appear timid and nervous.

As for my part, the effects of nitrogen at depth left me calm and fascinated during these meetings. On the long slow ascent to the surface after a particularly deep dive—during which a large gray reef shark had come very close, and lingered longer than usual—I began to realize the fragile nature of my situation. In my mouth was the electric taste of adrenaline that had flowed in response to the shark's behavior. It had been a futile attempt to get my nitrogen-inebriated mind to recognize the danger.

Although deep diving was thrilling, I was not finding as many new animals as I had hoped. I didn't yet realize it, but although I was looking for animals in a place few others did, I was still looking for them in the same way.

My real education began with the discovery of a little red cone shell, *Conus aurisiacus,* once one of the most valuable seashells in the world. Its great rarity made it a prize for collectors. This little cone shell was extremely rare, however, only until its habitat was discovered. Now *Conus aurisiacus* is one of the most common shells I know. Its habitat is so specific that a diver who knows the secret can find one literally in minutes, something difficult to do even with many common seashells. To those who know its habitat, this is a very common shell. To those who don't, it is as rare as it always has been. Habitat is the key.

I have discovered that many animals are considered rare not because there are only a few around, but because no one understands their habitat. Finding a particular animal is a matter of knowing where, or on what, it lives. And to locate new photographic subjects, my guiding principle has become: Find an unusual habitat and you will find unusual animals.

My addiction to the adventure and narcosis of depth passed as I realized the shallows were far richer than the deeper waters. Not only were there more species to photograph, there were far more habitats in which to look for new species. Shallow water also gave me much more bottom time to observe and photograph my subjects.

Diving shallow became a passion as strong as diving deep had been. I soon discovered that the turbid, lifeless waters I had been avoiding by traveling to the offshore islands were not lifeless at all. On my first mud bottom dive I saw an unusual, incredibly drab sea snake, several hauntingly blue gobies, and more varieties of venomous fish than I had ever seen before. It was a gold mine of new

BUNAKEN ISLAND, WITH MANADO TUA BEHIND

species. One problem remained, of course—that awful mud background.

Instead of looking for magnificent coral formations in crystal clear water I began looking for logs lying on mud in quiet, silty bays—sometimes right in front of villages or even cities. Like a reformed smoker, I swore off anything to do with deep, clear water.

This phase didn't last long. Mud diving is interesting, but not inspiring. Except for animals such as tilefish, blennies, gobies and a small assortment of interesting but ugly mud-dwelling fish like the stargazers, which can dive into the ooze to escape predators, most animals on mud bottoms were just passing through. Occasional logs provided temporary shelter for juvenile fish, but when they grew up they left.

And after several days and nights in 10 feet of water in the same trough, I began to yearn for a little visibility and maybe just a hint of current to carry off the silt lifted by my fins. A site just a little more attractive. I guess I was showing signs of moderation, a symptom of old age I had not yet encountered.

Arakan reef, southwest of Manado, offered good visibility and a plethora of micro-habitats. It also had wide expanses of relatively flat bottom, something I had come to appreciate. To dive at 50 feet on a wall you have to fol-

low a thin contour in one direction or the other. At Arakan the 50-foot contour was as wide as a barn, and choked with life. Visibility was a vast improvement over that encountered on my mud dives, and the bottom was white sand—not the light sucking grey-green of mud.

The reef structure at Arakan consists of patches of sand interspersed with formations of hard coral and sponges. Offshore the bottom rises in coral-covered mounds, islands of shallow water in an otherwise deep sea. Arakan, like the islands around Bunaken, is also a national marine reserve, and is home to an impressive array of invertebrates and small reef fish.

The animals I encountered at Arakan were completely different from those living on the mud bottom. Nor did I find a strong representation of the species living along the drop-offs of the Bunaken reserve. Of course there was some overlap with these other habitats, but Arakan mostly offered a collection of animals uniquely its own.

From the Nusantara Diving Centre on the coast north of Manado where we stayed, the trip to Arakan generally took all day, and required that we pass in front of the city of Manado. One night on our return we passed through the Manado fishing fleet in Manado Bay. The fleet consisted of hundreds of fragile outrigger canoes drifting in the still evening on calm seas, each with a lantern to attract fish and a fisherman endlessly pulling his line up at arm's length, then allowing it to sink back down. Though they were floating in very deep water, they were fishing just below the surface for a small sardine-like fish which was then dried for market.

I have always thought that the water reflecting the lights of a city at night is the blackest water of all. The reflection of all the lanterns, and of the lights of Manado in the distance, gave me an eerie feeling, and the water looked less inviting than it ever had before.

I long resisted the temptation to dive Manado Bay, but eventually succumbed in service of my hunt for the lowly seahorse, and of my wife's desire to see every living nudibranch within a ten-mile radius of her current position. We anchored in about four feet of water, put on our gear and rolled off the boat, striking the bottom with our tanks. Then we were picked up by the strong current and swept through a minefield of sea urchins and scorpionfish, over a bottom that offered no hand-holds at all.

Don't get me wrong. I am very glad to have made this dive. Now I can talk very knowingly about it if the subject ever comes up, and I have gained some leverage in future dive site discussions with Pauline.

FISHERMEN IN MANADO BAY

There was no real system to the way we approached diving in North Sulawesi. Where we dove on a particular day was decided by our whims and the weather. Often I would become interested in a subject and return to the same location day after day. When this happened it became difficult to keep diving partners, and even the ever social crew dwindled to the absolute minimum needed to insure our safe return.

Once, while snorkeling during a lunch break, I found a pair of male blue ribbon eels in shallow water on the reef flat. With a tank on my back and overweighted so I could lie on the bottom, I stayed well over two hours trying to get both eels in focus simultaneously. By the time I climbed back on the boat, all the food and what little common language existed between the crew and the other guests had long been exhausted. All that was left was a thick cloud of silence.

Over the years, Pauline and I gradually worked our way up the coast and around the tip of North Sulawesi, leaving the Sulawesi Sea and entering the Maluku Sea. As we did so the animals and available habitat changed until we were regularly seeing animals—such as anglerfish and certain butterflyfish—that previously had been rare. Even the lighting was different. The sun rose over the water on this east-facing coast, and the sunset cast the shadow of the mountains over the strait between Sulawesi's northeastern peninsula and Lembeh Island.

When we began diving North Sulawesi the Lembeh Strait area had no compressor, and the few divers who made the trip had to bring filled tanks from Manado. This was usually done only during the winter, when the weather made diving difficult around Bunaken. During the heavy winter rains, the port of Bitung and the Lembeh Strait remained calm. Even the rain was mostly blocked by the mountains of Sulawesi's northern peninsula.

Standing on the shores of the strait is like standing on the banks of a great saltwater river. It has always been calm when I've been there, and judging by how close to the water people have built their houses, it is seldom anything else. The only waves reaching shore are from passing boats. It is a very lovely and quiet place, a pleasant contrast to the bustle of Manado.

Though it is calm and quiet, there is a power to the strait in the strong current that flows through its channel. The Lembeh Strait acts as a lens, focusing the drifting planktonic larvae of countless species into a narrow body of water. Many simply pass through the long passage, sped on their way by the current. Others become trapped in eddies and bays, where they settle out to add to the diversity of life in the strait.

The Lembeh area offers shallow water with clean strong currents washing over the bottom, bringing plankton to the filter-feeders and continually depositing new animals. Here we found seahorses, blue-ringed octopus, unusual gobies and a rainbow of anglerfish, tunicates and soft corals. And all this in shallow water, and over a relatively flat bottom.

DAWN ON THE LEMBEH STRAIT

The Kungkungan Bay Resort has the only compressor in the area, and the bay in front of the resort has been a marine preserve since the property was purchased. It was from here that we completed the last phase of this book. The diving was varied and the bottom was so rich with animal species that I could find just about anything I needed without difficulty.

At the northern tip of Lembeh Island, just outside the mouth of the strait, is small Batu Kapal Island, which attracts big schools of jacks and barracuda, and is covered with colorful sponges and soft corals. Around the back side of Lembeh is Pulau Dua, where a steeply sloping white sand bottom reflects light onto beautiful isolated coral formations. The shallow waters of the strait itself are rich with rare animals, and its occasional small bays are full of the unusual mud-bottom animals I had first seen on the west coast of the peninsula.

One thing I learned early on about the people of North Sulawesi. If you make a request, they will almost never say no—even if they know they can't honor it. "No" is just too rude. When I asked one of the guides to show me where I could find a seahorse, he said, "Tomorrow." Great, I thought, but everyone felt severe embarrassment the next

MANGROVES IN FRONT OF MOLAS VILLAGE, NEAR MANADO

PAULINE FIENE-SEVERNS

day—and no one more so than me—when I crudely brought up the subject after no seahorse was found. It is a delightful, but frustrating, trait.

So, many years later, I was prepared when I asked Engel Lumakeki, the boat captain at Kungkungan, to help me find a seahorse. We spent three full days snorkeling, diving and generally baking in the boat while looking in all the places he thought we might find one of these frustratingly elusive creatures. Finally, after many hours poking around in shallow back bays and being stared at in naked wonderment by local fishermen, we gave up.

Then one evening, just before dark, Engel found a seahorse. It was swimming in eight inches of water, directly in front of our cottage. Everyone was thrilled—except, of course, the seahorse, which is no doubt still recovering from the worst storm of strobe flashes it has ever seen. The next morning there were two more in the same place.

Buoyed by this success, I asked Engel where I might find a blue-ringed octopus. Now I'm a little slow sometimes figuring out what's happening around me, but Engel isn't. He pointed to the pier in front of the resort. The water there is only six feet deep, but he had seen the type of octopus I was looking for there on a piling.

Only later was I able to put his answer in perspective. Of course, If I dove at the pier I wouldn't require Engel's boat, nor would Engel have to bake in the hot sun for three or four days in various isolated back bays of the strait. Perhaps this is why he didn't at first add that it was several years ago that he saw the octopus under the pier.

Every evening, after everyone one else had cleaned their gear and headed for the shower, I would wade into the water and slip beneath the pier in the waning light to look for a blue-ringed octopus. I spent days at this routine, watching the barnacles on the pier pilings feed, and trying to avoid a pair of wasp scorpion fish that had become so used to my presence in their territory that they looked at me as substrate.

Then, a very stiff, very water-logged photographer saw something he had not even imagined. I was watching a small crab when, seemingly out of nowhere, a small octopus struck and covered the crab with its skirt.

It wasn't until it had the crab in its arms that it began to pulsate, displaying bright blue rings. When not agitated the octopus had remained very cryptic, and was invisible as it moved toward its prey. After the strike, it glowed with confidence, and flashed a warning not to be bothered. The blue rings eventually faded, the ground color darkened, and a little green circle appeared within the blue rings. Then the little octopus gathered up its now paralyzed catch and carried it past me as if I were a tree in its path. It was obviously very familiar with me.

One day while decompressing after diving on one of the strait's wrecks, I noticed a drifting sea-grass stem that seemed to continually move away from me. This attracted my attention, and then I noticed two thumb-sized baby jacks swimming beside the grass. I still hadn't caught on, however, until suddenly I noticed that this "grass" had two eyes. It also had a brain and could definitely swim, and every time I even looked like I was going to pull the trigger on my camera, it turned away. This strange subject was a small pipefish that had wrapped its tail around a piece of drifting turtle grass. It was the same color and thickness as the grass, but unlike grass, possessed a definite aversion to having its picture taken.

There is no place in North Sulawesi that I would recommend more than the Lembeh Strait. There is enough diving and as many different habitats as anyone could ask for. The diving here is among the richest in the world for reef life, which is what this book is all about.

In photographing Sulawesi Seas, I have been very strict about shooting the animals exactly as I found them, with-

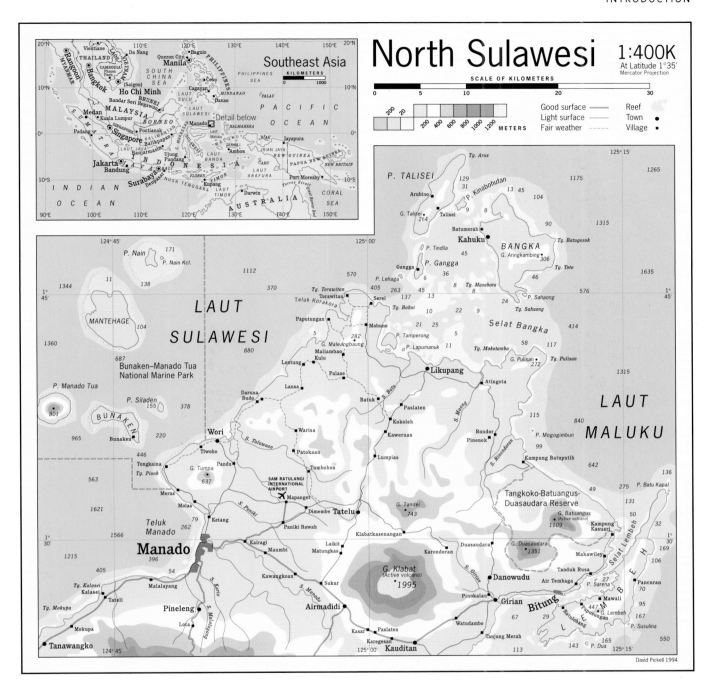

out touching or disturbing them at all. This is not always easy, or even possible, and I have made two exceptions. One was *Octopus horridus,* which was such a rare animal that I just had to get a good shot of it away from the gravelly bottom. In the end, I gently lifted it free of the bottom and shot it in the water column. The other was the chambered nautilus, which was captured in a baited trap set deep in the water, held in a bucket packed in ice, and then released in blue water. I photographed it as it descended the abyss. At a bit over 200 feet I stopped taking pictures, and watched it continue down into the cold, dark world I had brought it from hours before.

The photograph of the hatching cuttlefish is the type of shot that is normally done in a laboratory, and shooting it in situ made it probably the most difficult shot in this book. The photograph was taken at sunset, in six feet of water, right where the eggs were attached by the female cuttlefish. When the newborn cuttlefish darted off, it went exactly where it would have had I not been there to witness the event.

One of my greatest pleasures in photographing in North Sulawesi has been the people who live here. Every last one of them is a character, and they are without a doubt the loveliest people I have ever worked with.

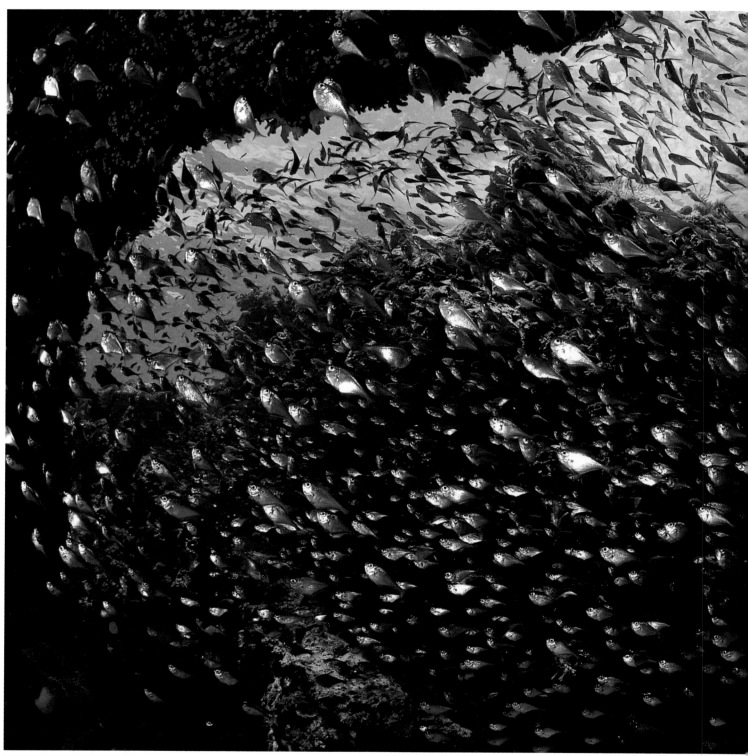

SWEEPERS: PEMPHERIS OUALENSIS

Copper sweepers fill this small cave during the day. At night they disperse from these large schools and forage individually over the reef, returning the next morning to caves and surge channels, and the protection of the group.

FILEFISH: BRACHALUTERES TAYLORI   GORGONIAN: EUPLEXAURA SP.

BLENNY: MEIACANTHUS ATRODORSALIS

The tiny Taylor's inflator filefish at left combines the defenses of both puffers and filefish. If threatened, this inch-long fish can swallow water and inflate its body like a puffer, and erect its stiff dorsal spine like a filefish. Either or both of these actions will increase its apparent size, which—particularly when performed suddenly—can startle and discourage a would-be predator.

This yellowtail fangblenny rests among the branches of a sponge at night. Thanks to its formidable defenses, by day it has no need to hide, and can be seen out in the open plucking small crustaceans and other plankters from the current. The blenny carries two large, grooved fangs in its lower jaw, each with a venom gland at its base. Its bite has been compared to the sting of a wasp, although the fangs are used only in defense. The fangblenny's reputation is such that several other species mimic its coloration and movements, and are thus unmolested.

TUNICATES: CLAVELINA SP.

A brief, free-swimming larval stage is all the freedom these tunicates have ever known. In just minutes, the newly hatched, tadpole-like larvae seek the substrate by swimming away from the light, then attach and metamorphose into adult tunicates. Because the larvae have notocords, a kind of primitive backbone, tunicates are actually chordates, and are classed in the same phylum as human beings and all other vertebrates. Tunicates are unique in the animal kingdom in that their adult form is simpler than that of their larvae.

Green algae harbor numerous species of sacoglossans, shell-less molluscs related to nudibranchs. Most of them are brilliant green in color, which disguises their presence. These feed by puncturing the liquid-filled sacs of the alga with a single tooth, and then drawing out the contents with a muscular pump. The animals retain the chloroplasts from the alga in their skin, and these continue to photosynthesize, providing another source of nutrition for the sacoglossans.

SACOGLOSSANS: PETALIFERA RAMOSA   ALGA: CAULERPA RACEMOSA

ANGELFISH: POMACANTHUS IMPERATOR (JUVENILE)

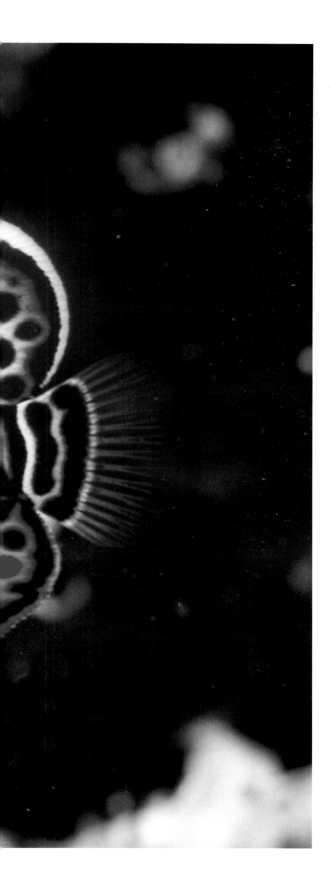

ANGELFISH: POMACANTHUS IMPERATOR (ADULT)

The effectiveness of the juvenile emperor angelfish's dizzying defensive coloration becomes obvious to anyone who tries to look at it for long. The op-art stripes are lost as the fish matures, to be replaced by an equally beautiful, but less disturbing pattern. Although as adults they are quite distinct, all Indo-Pacific angelfishes of this genus have similar juvenile patterns.

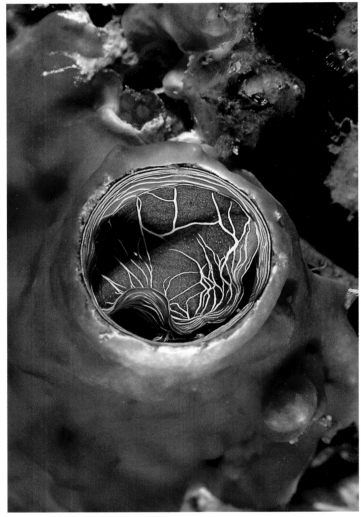

WORM MOLLUSC: DENDROPOMA MAXIMA

Though it resembles a worm, the animal pictured above is a type of snail called a worm mollusc. It secretes a tubular shell which remains attached to the bottom and feeds by spinning out mucous threads. When these sticky threads become laden with organic material, it hauls them in and ingests its "catch."

At first glance, these animals appear to be flatworms, but in fact they are an unusual type of ctenophore. Most ctenophores—often called comb jellies—are transparent, open ocean swimmers, but a few have adapted to a creeping existence. These are living on the belly of a sea cucumber.

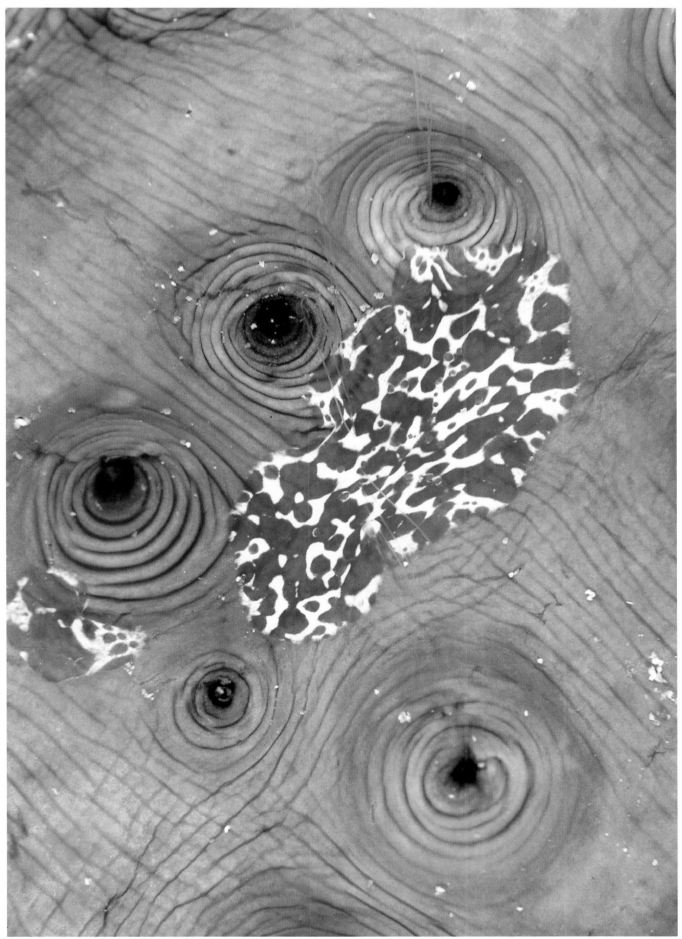

CTENOPHORES: COELOPLANA SP.   SEA CUCUMBER: STICHOPUS SP.

A glass-calm sea allowed this perfect reflection of shallow water corals, and a strange image we call: "No Way Out."

FLATWORM: PSEUDOCEROS DIMIDIATUS   NUDIBRANCH: CHROMODORIS SP.

30

WRASSE: CORIS AYGULA

Brightly colored flatworms can be seen feeding openly during the day, relying on light detecting patches of tissue on their backs to sense their way, and their strong and adhesive bellies to crawl about. Although they would make exceptionally easy prey, no animal will touch them. They are quite toxic, a fact advertised by their bright colors. Like many of the most beautifully patterned marine flatworms, this species is ordered in a group called the polyclads. Also visible in this photograph, curled in a cranny in the sponge, is a small lavender and orange chromodorid nudibranch.

While still a juvenile, the clown wrasse wears bright colors and two large eye-spots, which confuse predators. When it matures, it will lose the spots and assume a more somber coloration, mostly shades of gray and black.

SHRIMP: PERICLIMENES COMMENSALIS

These two shrimp are the same species, yet since each has been able to closely duplicate the color of its host crinoid, both are extremely difficult to see. When a larval shrimp settles out of the plankton stream onto a crinoid, it quickly adopts the color of its host. If all goes well, the shrimp and crinoid will be partners for life. If the shrimp finds itself in need of a new host, it can once again change its color to match.

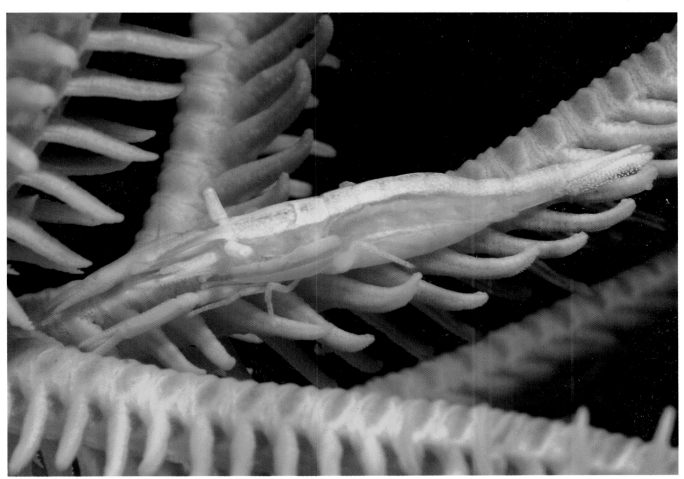

SHRIMP: PERICLIMENES COMMENSALIS

GHOST PIPEFISH: SOLENOSTOMUS PARADOXUS

SEA MOTH: PEGASUS VOLITANS

Photographing the ornate ghost pipefish at left was an ordeal, as no matter where I positioned my camera, she turned her belly away, keeping her clutch of eggs away from me and near the protection of the gorgonian. Unlike true pipefish, among which the males incubate the eggs, the female ghost pipefish keeps her silvery eggs in a little pouch she creates by clasping together her ventral fins and hooking them to her body.

The curious sea moth lives in shallow water, where it searches for small invertebrates over sandy or muddy bottoms. Except where the tail and abdomen need to bend, the sea moth's body is entirely shielded in bony plates. As I watched, this one worked its way across the bottom in small steps, occasionally pecking at minute crustaceans in its path. Despite my presence, it appeared not to be overly concerned for its safety. I have heard that the sea moth gives off a strong odor when removed from the water, although I decided not to test this myself.

FUSILIERS: CAESIO SP.   GORGONIAN: FAMILY PLEXAURIDAE

A squad of fusiliers swings past a large gorgonian on the reef edge. During the day they patrol the reef edges in schools, feeding on plankton, but at night each finds a protected hiding place on the reef.

The growth strategy of this table coral yields numerous benefits for the colonial animals within its calcium skeleton. The horizontal structure efficiently exposes the photosynthetic algae in the coral's tissues to the light, and when growing on the reef edge, as here, the colony can grow outward and take advantage of space that is simply not available to vertical-growing corals.

CORAL: ACROPORA HYACINTHUS

UNIDENTIFIED SHRIMP

GOBY: BRYANINOPS YONGEI   WIRE CORAL: CIRRIPATHES ANGUINA

Several species of commensal shrimp live on crinoids, benefiting from the protection provided by their colorful hosts. Just below the shrimp, in the center of the oral surface, is the crinoid's raised mouth.

Yonge's wire coral goby glides up and down the length of the wire coral, looking for particles of food drifting by in the water. The way these little fish stick to the black coral strand is remarkable, as if some kind of magnetic force is at work. The orange transverse bands visually disrupt the shape of the goby's body, helping it to blend in with its host.

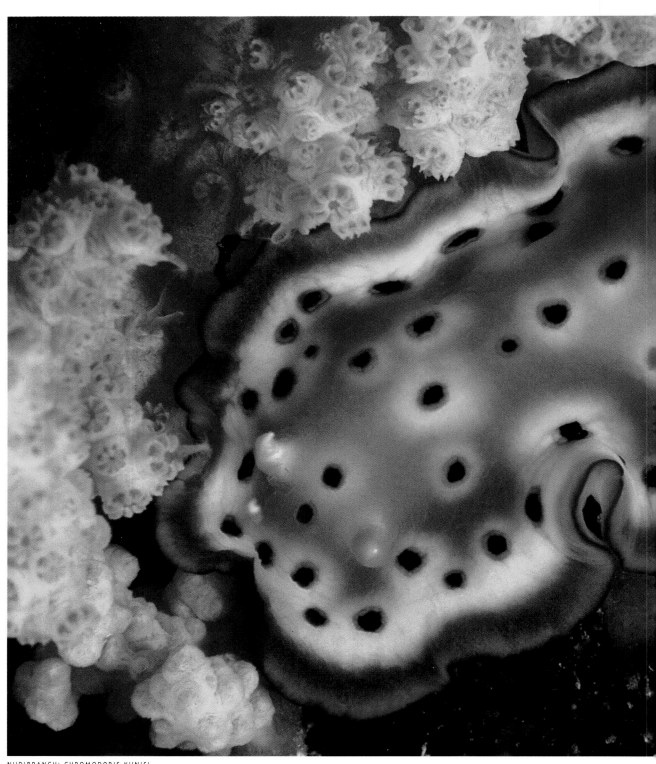

NUDIBRANCH: CHROMODORIS KUNIEI

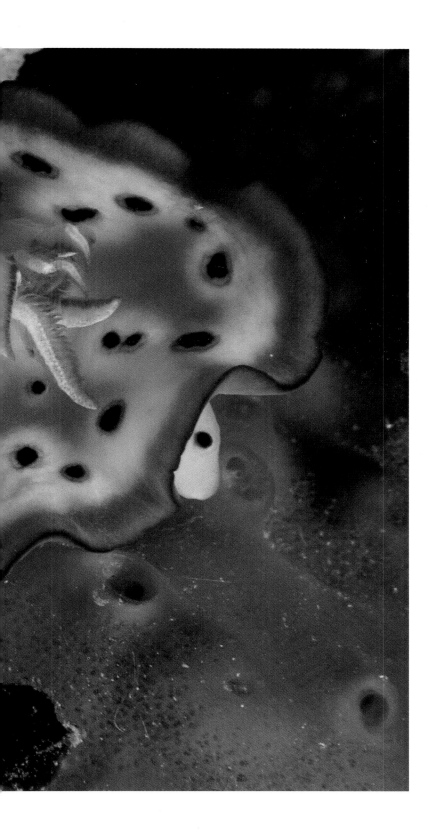

Loud coloration in nudibranchs, like in many other animals, is often a warning to would-be predators that the animal is distasteful. Inexperienced fish that eat toxic nudibranchs will spit them out, learn from the experience, and avoid them in the future. This chromodorid nudibranch, like others in its genus, feeds on sponges.

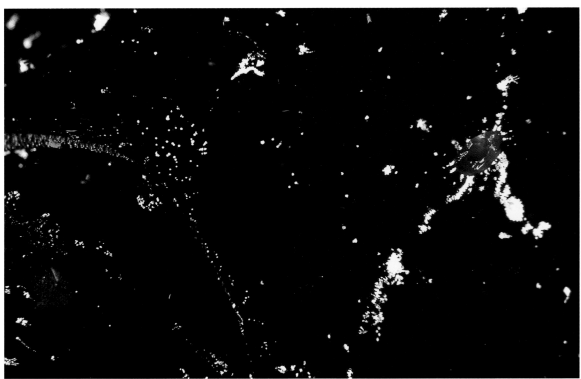

ANGLERFISH: ANTENNARIUS PICTUS

Flecks of white pigment and particles of silt shine like stars against the coal black skin of the large angler-fish above. An anglerfish's lumpy shape is already difficult to see when motionless against the bottom, but this individual, as lightless as a shadow, is just about invisible.

Peering with my lens through the massive siphon of this giant clam, I noticed that its gills had provided a habitat for a tiny shrimp. Although miniscule, the giant clam shrimp has large claws, as what to a normal-sized shrimp is merely a speck of zooplankton, to this little one could be a real threat.

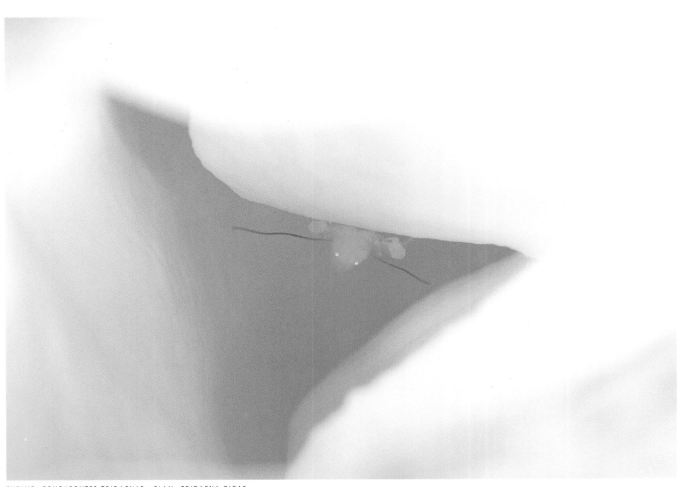
SHRIMP: CONCHODYTES TRIDACNAE   CLAM: TRIDACNA GIGAS

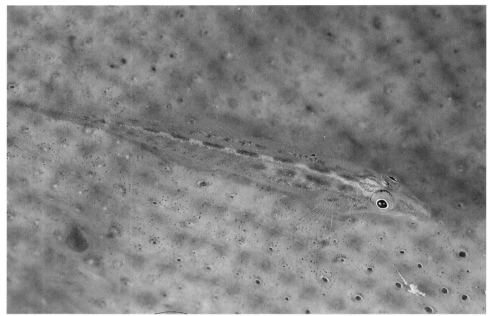
GOBY: PLEUROSICYA ELONGATA

I found this cling goby on the inner surface of a leathery sponge growing in the shallow, almost milky water of the back reef flat. The goby preys on any small invertebrates that come within range, then retreats to the interior of the sponge, the atrium, where its matching coloration provides it some protection.

Jacks hunt individually at night, but during the day they return to the same location, forming dense schools for protection. Generally these schools can be found along reef walls in areas of strong current. The school hovers in an eddy, and is ready to spill out into a huge swarm if alarmed, or if its curiosity is aroused.

JACKS: CARANX SEXFASCIATUS

EELS: RHINOMURAENA QUAESITA

EEL: RHINOMURAENA QUAESITA

During the day this pair of male ribbon eels sought the protection of the same hole in the reef, but at night they will leave to forage individually for small fish in the shallows. The ribbon eel is a protandrous hermaphrodite—all individuals mature first as males, and then some sex-change to females. This sex change is marked by a dramatic change in color: sexually immature eels are black, mature males are blue and females are yellow. I have seen many males, but the female above is the only one I have ever encountered. She was very timid, and her light color made her hard to see against the sand.

TUNICATE: RHOPALAEA SP.

WORM: SPIROBRANCHUS GIGANTEUS

The transparent tunic of this crystalline tunicate, or sea squirt, allows us to see inside to the tubular body wall, which has many tiny perforations for filtering water. Water drawn in through the top siphon is strained of plankton and organic particles by mucous webs strung across the tiny holes and then ejected through the siphon facing us.

The pair of delicate respiratory structures protruding from the tube of this Christmas tree worm appear to be an easy meal for a passing fish, but the worm is very quick. When it senses even a subtle change in light or current, it pulls in the fans and snaps its trap door shut. A fish that attacks, and is too slow for the worm, faces an unpleasant encounter with a sharp spine at the entrance to the tube.

SEA URCHIN: TRIPNEUSTES GRATILLA ALGA: HALIMEDA OPUNTIA

This sea urchin creeps through the canopy of an algae forest by using its long tube feet to pull nearby strands close enough to transfer to a new perch. Using this method, it can cover many feet without touching bottom. The thick calcium carbonate–reinforced disks of the algae shield the urchin, forming a first line of defense against tough-mouthed fish like triggerfish, which could otherwise attack and break the urchin's fragile shell.

Poised for a strike, this blotched hawkfish perches in a gorgonian and waits for small fish and crustaceans to swim within range. The thickened rays of its pectoral fins allow it to hold the branches firmly, and to launch in a split-second. Since they do not possess a swim bladder, hawkfish are negatively buoyant underwater. This helps them swoop down on their prey with greater speed and force.

HAWKFISH: CIRRHITICHTHYS APRINUS

ANEMONEFISH: AMPHIPRION SANDARACINOS   SEA ANEMONE: STICHODACTYLA MERTENSII

ANEMONEFISH: AMPHIPRION POLYMNUS   DAMSELFISH: DASCYLLUS TRIMACULATUS   ANEMONE: STICHODACTYLA HADDONI

The sting of Merten's anemone, the largest of all sea anemones, is quite potent, but the orange skunk clownfish at left is obviously immune. It can snuggle in the stinging tentacles because of the special nature of its mucus coating which, through some combination of the fish's own biochemistry and a material picked up from the anemone itself, does not trigger the deadly nematocyst cells to fire. The protection of the anemone is essential to the clownfish, which is a poor swimmer and in the open would soon be eaten.

This large Haddon's anemone is a hub of activity, hosting more than 20 fish. Each of these large and small saddleback anemonefish has a place in a hierarchy dominated by a single breeding pair. Sharing the host with the saddleback anemonefish are immature three-spot dascyllus, which use the anemone for protection only when young, and even then avoid direct contact with its tentacles.

SHRIMP: PERICLIMENES IMPERATOR   NUDIBRANCH: DENDRODORIS TUBERCULOSA

This imperial shrimp shelters in a cave formed by the frond-like gills of a large tuberculated nudibranch. The convoluted texture of the nudibranch's body provides a maze of protection for the shrimp, which lives here with its mate. I took this photograph at night, and my lights attracted a swarm of tiny shrimp-like mysids. As I watched, the imperial shrimp deftly snatched one in its claw.

CORAL: ACROPORA SP.

Corals of the genus *Acropora*, the largest and most important group of reef-building corals, can assume many different growth forms: small clumps, bushes, large branches and tables. Large tables like these, growing in the shallow reef flat in front of Manado Tua, efficiently expose the living animals to sunlight, and by building the colony horizontally, this fast-growing species quickly chokes out any would-be competitors.

CORAL: SINULARIA FLEXIBILIS

This soft coral prefers the shallow, protected waters of the back reef. The coral's tissues harbor photosynthetic algae which benefit from the strong sunlight. Soft corals like this one are often more tolerant than hard corals of the warm, turbid, nutrient-rich water of the section of the reef adjoining the mangroves.

NUDIBRANCH: NEMBROTHA LIVINGSTONEI

NUDIBRANCH: NEMBROTHA CRISTATA

Nudibranchs are so little-studied that the known range for many consists of a mere patchwork of scattered sightings. The species at left has so far been identified in just three very wide-ranging locations: Southern Africa, Western Australia and North Sulawesi. Its true range is certainly more extensive than this.

Although they are often observed on their prey items, the beauty of the nudibranch often so outshines that of its prey that the latter goes unnoticed. It is quite obvious what this *Nembrotha* likes to eat, however: the chewy ball of a compound tunicate.

OCTOPUS: OCTOPUS HORRIDUS COMPLEX

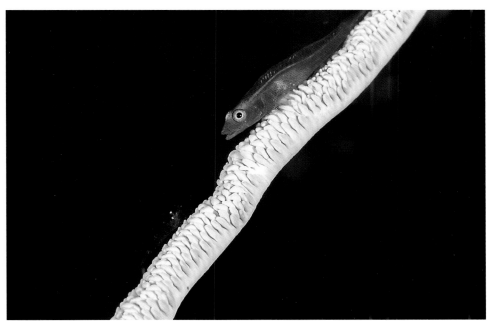

GOBY: BRYANINOPS SP.   SHRIMP: PONTONIDES SP.   WIRE CORAL: CIRRIPATHES ANGUINA

Wire coral gobies are poor swimmers, but by clinging to the whip-like strands of antipatharian coral with specially modified pelvic fins, they can feed in the fast-moving currents. The small shrimp facing the goby probably helps clean both the coral and the goby of parasites.

The octopus opposite is a member of a very poorly understood group of shallow water octopus. It is a bottom dweller that I have seen only on a coarse sand substrate, and is so rare that fewer than a dozen specimens are known to have been studied. These octopus are remarkable and instantaneous mimics, and can even produce an almost believable approximation of a lionfish. So little is known of this complex of octopus that the potential effects of its venom on humans is still a mystery.

ANGELFISH: APOLEMICHTHYS TRIMACULATUS

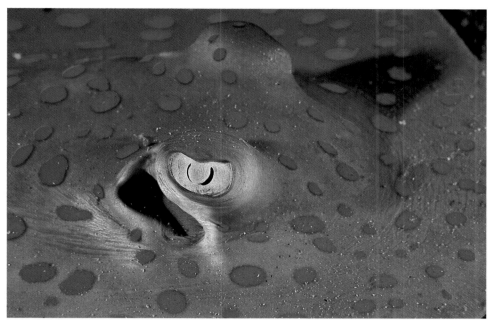
RAY: TAENIURA LYMMA

This three-spot angelfish was a real character. Instead of running away from me as all the others had, it kept circling behind a rock, each time returning to the same spot to watch me. Eventually I figured out the game, and beat him to it. These fish eat sponges and tunicates and are unaffected by the toxins contained in them.

The blue-spotted stingray is by far the most common ray we see around North Sulawesi, lurking under coral ledges or in caves. These rays feed in the open over patches of sand, flapping their "wings" to uncover hidden molluscs and worms.

PIPEFISH: SYNGNATHOIDES BIACULEATUS

While decompressing after a long dive near Bitung, I idly watched a small piece of grass drift past, turning slowly in the current. This pipefish's maneuvers to keep the grass directly between it and me were so subtle that I hadn't noticed it at first, until I saw its eyes. Holding onto the drifting grass with its tail, this fish disguised itself as the very shelter its minute prey would seek in the open water. Parasitic isopods have attached themselves to the little pipefish's chin and forehead.

This spectacular creature is a juvenile pinnate batfish. Adults of this species are a dull silver color, and have a pointed snout and less extravagent finnage. The juvenile's striking coloration is thought to mimic that of a toxic Pseudocerid flatworm. This individual is very young, and not much bigger than a silver dollar. As it grows larger, its fins will elongate, better matching the proportions of a flatworm.

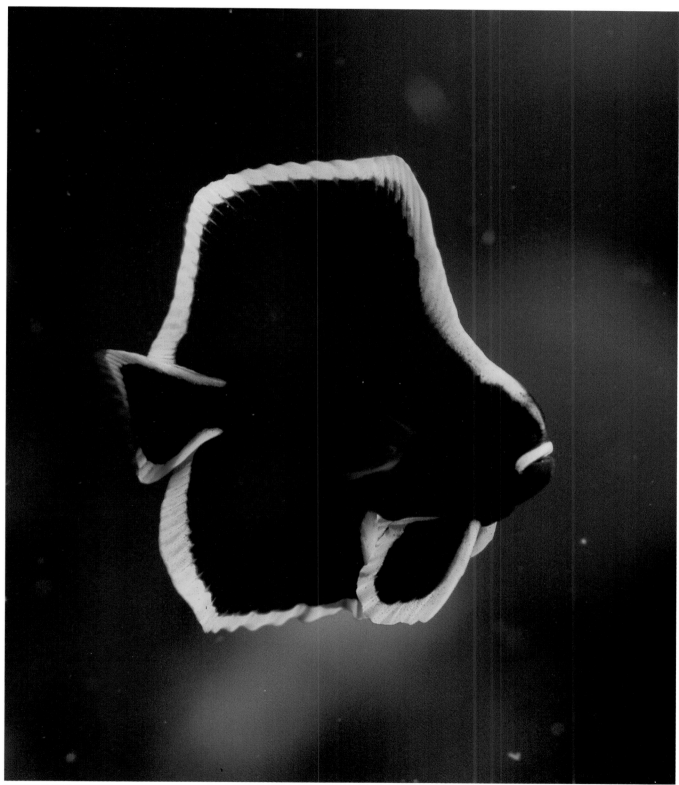

BATFISH: PLATAX PINNATUS

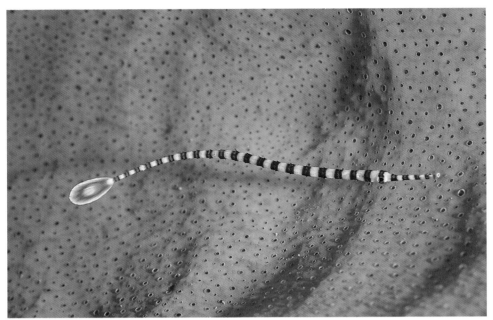

PIPEFISH: DORYRHAMPHUS (DUNKEROCAMPUS) DACTYLIOPHORUS

The banded pipefish above is common in shallow protected water along the shoreline, where it feeds on plankton. This individual was living on the outer surface of a sponge, probably snapping up planktonic organisms that were drawn to the sponge by the current produced by its ciliated cells.

The long flexible body of the network pipefish allows it to conform to the bottom or, as here, to a protective soft coral colony. This species is extremely common in North Sulawesi, and during the day individuals can be seen feeding on microcrustaceans in the still, shallow waters of back reefs and bays.

PIPEFISH: CORYTHOICHTHYS FLAVOFASCIATUS   CORAL: LOBOPHYTUM SP.

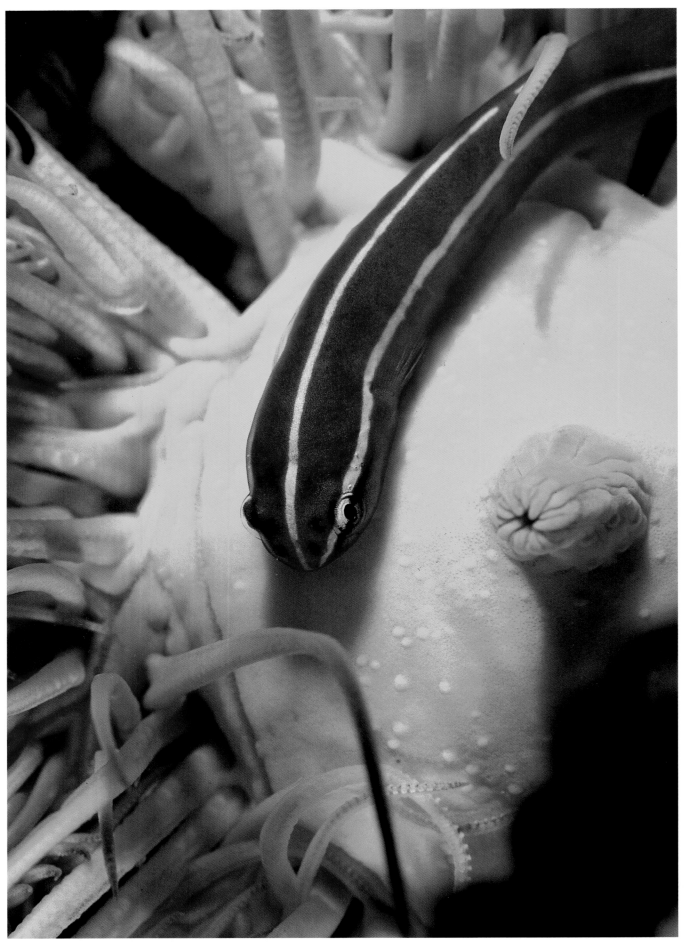

CLINGFISH: DISCOTREMA ECHINOPHILA

JAWFISH: OPISTOGNATHUS RANDALLI

As I watched, the clingfish at left climbed onto the top of the crinoid and chased two smaller yellow clingfish to its underside. It was evening, and this little drama was probably part of the fishes' daily routine. Clingfish often seek protection among the arms of crinoids, using a suction cup formed of highly modified pelvic fins to cling to their host.

The mouth of this jawfish is strong enough to move rocks and scoop out a burrow, but also gentle enough to incubate a clutch of eggs. The embryos here are close to hatching, and their fully developed eyes can be seen reflecting light.

DARTFISH: NEMATELEOTRIS DECORA

In areas of the reef with strong currents, pairs or small groups of decorated dartfish can be found hovering above the bottom, feeding on drifting plankton. When alerted to danger, these high-strung fish will dart over to just above an already prepared refuge in the bottom, and hover nervously. When the threat becomes intolerable, the fish dive into the hole, and wait there patiently until all signs of danger have passed.

This purple queen fairy basslet is being checked for parasites by a small cleaner wrasse. The basslet's trust in the wrasse is so complete that it allows it to clean the extremely sensitive tissue around its eye. Cleaning generally occurs in the fading light of late afternoon, and the fish become so engrossed in the activity that they are easily approached.

FAIRY BASSLET: PSEUDANTHIAS TUKA   WRASSE: LABROIDES DIMIDIATUS

TRUMPETFISH: AULOSTOMUS CHINENSIS

ANEMONEFISH: PREMNAS BIACULEATUS   SEA ANEMONE: ENTACMAEA QUADRICOLOR

The night photograph at left shows a young trumpetfish sleeping among the arms of a crinoid. During the day this fish will lurk among corals and crinoids, disguising its long, streamlined shape. When prey approaches, usually a small fish, the trumpetfish shoots forward with a powerful lash of its tail. Its expanding mouth is well ahead of the pulse created by the tail, and this surprises the prey, which may have deduced the trumpet-fish's speed, but not its true distance.

The spine-cheeked anemonefish is the largest of all anemonefish, and the only member of its genus. The colors of this fish vary from orange to maroon to almost black, and only occasionally is it as flagrantly red as this one. When it comes to its choice of host, the spine-cheeked anemonefish is one of the pickiest of its kind, accepting only the bulb-tentacled anemone.

UNIDENTIFIED CRINOID

CORAL: TURBINARIA PELTATA

The crinoid at left grips the lip of a coral colony and extends its ten branched arms to strain plankton from the water. Plankton and organic matter adhere to mucous on the crinoid's arms, and are carried down to the central mouth and digested.

This common hard coral has very large polyps, which makes it easy to mistake for a soft coral. Like some other corals, *Turbinaria* assumes different growth forms depending on local conditions. In the shallows, as here, it grows in flat, twisted plates; In deeper water, it assumes a lumpy, massive shape. This reef-building coral is one of the few whose range extends beyond the tropics, reaching as far north as Japan, and as far south as south-western Australia.

SQUAT LOBSTER: ALLOGALATHEA ELEGANS

Crinoids shelter many unusual creatures like the elegant squat lobster above. The squat lobster and the crinoid share a symbiotic relationship—the squat lobster defends the crinoid against potential predators and helps rid it of parasites, and the crinoid offers the shelter of its feathery arms. The color and pattern of the squat lobster can change to match those of its host crinoid.

Communication among nudibranchs of the same species has nothing to do with their visual perception of each other's distinctive colors, because nudibranch eyes function, at best, as light/dark receptors. This nudibranch will find a mate by tracking emitted chemical signals with its pair of rhinophores. As yet undescribed, the species pictured here differs from most known chromodorids by possessing transverse bands of color.

NUDIBRANCH: UNDESCRIBED CHROMODORIS SP.

NAUTILUS: NAUTILUS POMPILIUS

The nautilus, a strange relative of octopus, squid and cuttlefish, is one of the most mysterious animals in nature. Its chambered shell serves as a complex buoyancy control device, which serves it well in its daily migration from cold, near abyssal depths during the day to relatively shallow water—although still hundreds of feet deep—at night to feed. To photograph this specimen, I had to first trap it from a depth of more than 300 feet. Local fishermen, using wooden canoes like the one pictured at left, set the traps out past the reef edge. The animals are somewhat frail and very sensitive to warm water, so I kept this one in a bucket packed in ice on the way to the dive site. Then I released it along the reef wall, photographing it as it headed slowly back down into the dark, cold water from which it had come just hours before.

ANEMONEFISH: AMPHIPRION CLARKII SEA ANEMONE: ENTACMAEA QUADRICOLOR

ANEMONEFISH: AMPHIPRION POLYMNUS   SHRIMP: PERICLIMENES SP.
SEA ANEMONE: STICHODACTYLA HADDONI

The juvenile Clark's anemonefish at left are dwarfed by the unique bulbous tentacles of their host. Colonies of anemonefish consist of two sexually mature adults, a male and a larger female, and a few to dozens of juveniles like these. If either member of the reigning pair is killed by a predator, the largest of the juveniles will quickly increase in size and become the sexually active male. Until this event, however, the juveniles are kept stunted by aggression down the pecking order.

Late one afternoon, as I watched these saddleback anemonefish begin to settle into their host anemone, cleaner shrimp, which normally hide among the anemone's tentacles, straddled the fish and began cleaning them. During the day the fish hover above the anemone to feed, and occasionally can become host to unwanted parasites which attach to their skin.

PIPEFISH: DORYRHAMPHUS EXCISUS   TUNICATE: POLYCARPA AURATA

BLENNY: PLAGIOTREMUS RHINORHYNCHOS   TUNICATE: POLYCARPA AURATA

The bluestripe pipefish at left is small and inconspicuous, living in isolated coral formations. It swims with a distinctive bobbing motion,
similar to the dance of cleaner wrasses, which advertises to larger fish
and eels that the pipefish, too, is a cleaner.

This bluestripe fangblenny watches for prey while safely sheathed in an
empty worm mollusc tube. When a larger fish passes by, the blenny
darts out and rips off a chunk of mucous, skin and even scales. Before
its victim can exact revenge, the blenny whisks back to its lair and
slides, tail first, to safety.

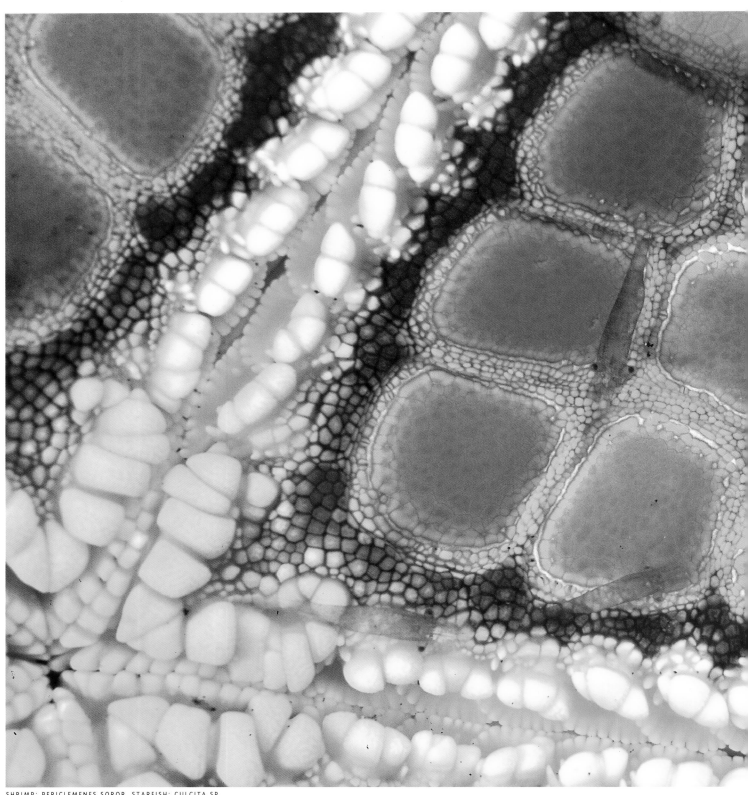

SHRIMP: PERICLEMENES SOROR STARFISH: CULCITA SP.

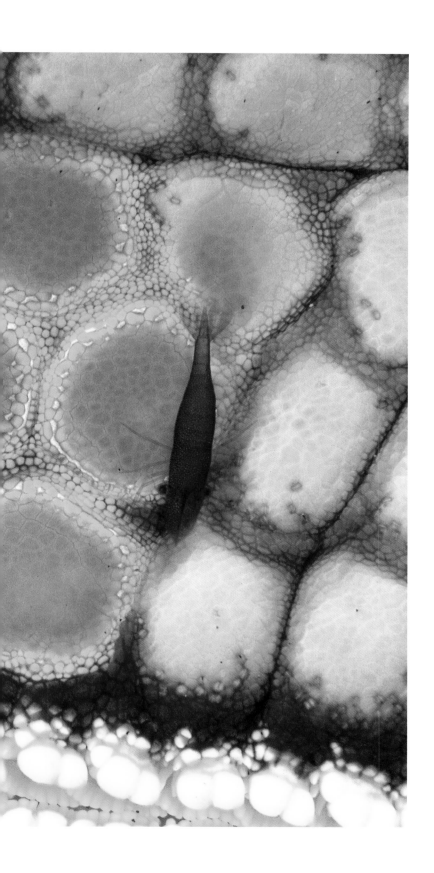

From their cleanly tiled living space on the bottom of a cushion starfish, these shrimp can feed in safety, hidden from view. As the starfish moves about the reef, the shrimp can take advantage of new feeding territory without having to change residence, sometimes climbing on top the starfish to eat the organic material caught on the starfish's short spines and papillae. Venturing from beneath the starfish is risky, however, and I saw a sand goby mount a starfish, snatch a shrimp, and swim off with its catch sideways in its mouth.

UNIDENTIFIED CERIANTHID

CUTTLEFISH: SEPIA LATIMANUS

The long tentacles of this cerianthid, or tube anemone, reach far out into the water to snare plankton, which is then transferred to the shorter tentacles in the center, and eventually to the mouth. A layer of sticky mucous prevents the food from being lost in the transaction. Tube anemones, related to anemones and corals, secrete leathery tubes which are buried in the substrate. If harassed, they will quickly withdraw into this shelter.

The giant cuttlefish, closely related to the squids, is the most curious and personable invertebrate a diver will meet on the reef. The cuttlefish is also a subtle and formidable hunter, and by suddenly shooting out its tentacles can snatch a swimming fish almost twice its body length away.

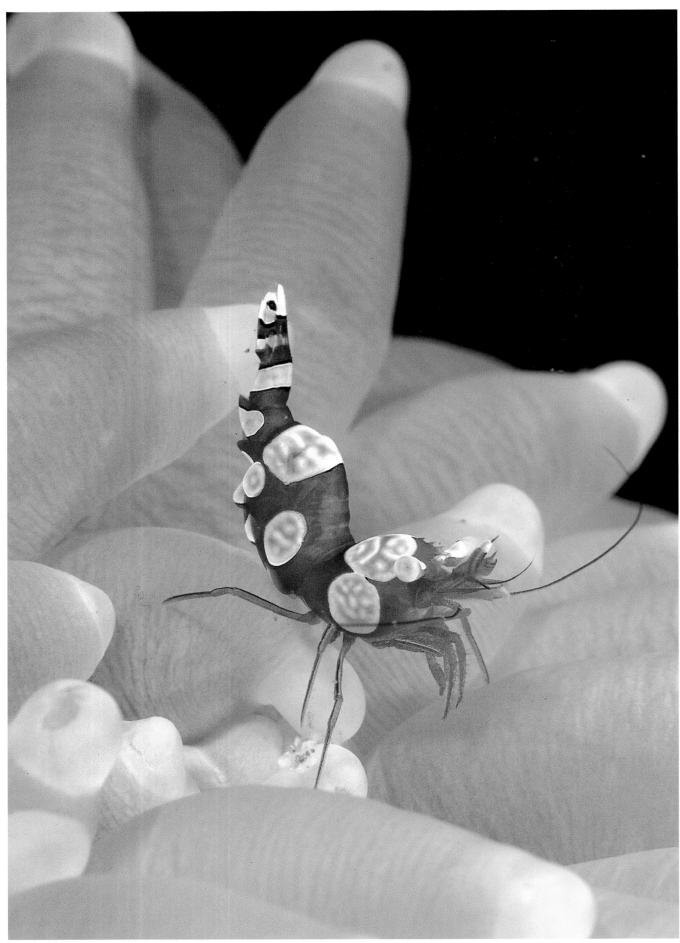

SHRIMP: THOR AMBOINENSIS CORAL: HELIOFUNGIA ACTINIFORMIS

SHRIMP: PERICLIMENES HOLTHUISI SEA ANEMONE: HETERACTIS MAGNIFICA

Though it looks like an anemone, the tentacles at left actually extend from the hard, calcareous skeleton of a mushroom coral. Like a sea anemone, however, the coral has venomous stinging cells and this shrimp has taken advantage of the protection they offer. Although not as mobile as anemones, mushroom corals are capable of limited movement, such as gradually righting themselves if knocked over by a storm, or pulling themselves out if buried in sand.

The remarkable clarity of this commensal shrimp's body is part of its defense. It is a cleaner, and when it wishes to attract attention, the shrimp hovers slightly above its host anemone or rests on the tips of the anemone's tentacles and sways back and forth. When it feels the need to hide, it simply remains still, its transparent body making it practically invisible against the mass of tentacles. Note that this female shrimp is gravid with a clutch of pink eggs.

MANDARINFISH: SYNCHIROPUS SPLENDIDUS

In the photograph above a large female mandarinfish is being nuzzled in courtship by a smaller male. He wasn't the only suitor—at least three other males made similar passes at the hovering female. These very colorful fish live in extremely small territories and are not often seen by divers.

Without question this is one of the most beautiful species of shrimp I have seen, and living on one of the most beautiful sea urchins. I found the urchin on a mud bottom, and very deep. The Coleman's shrimp live in the furrows between the spines and did not move at all as I photographed them. I could also count on finding the urchin day after day in exactly the same place—if, that is, I was able to find the spot again on such a featureless bottom. The larger of the two shrimp is the female.

SHRIMP: PERICLIMENES COLEMANI   SEA URCHIN: ASTHENOSOMA INTERMEDIUM

BANNERFISH: HENIOCHUS CHRYSOSTOMUS

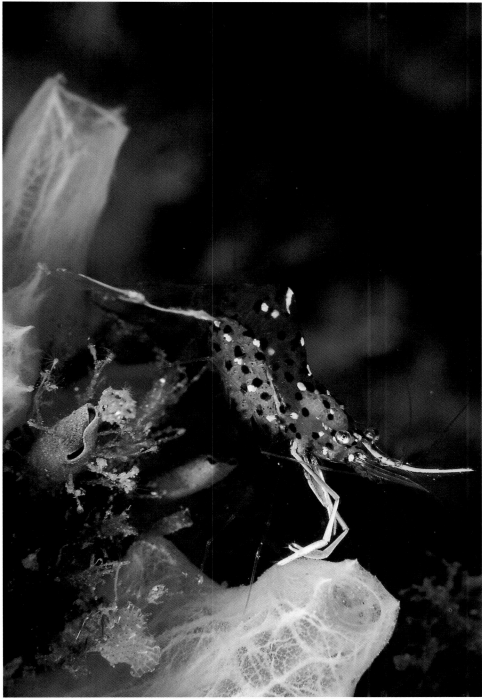

SHRIMP: RHYNCHOCINETES SP.

The bannerfish at left feeds primarily on coral polyps, using its delicate mouth and brush-like teeth to pluck the animals from their stony cups. Unlike some butterflyfish, this species travels about the reef alone.

The distinct black eye spots suggest that the batch of eggs held by this beaked shrimp are almost ready to hatch. In fact, a new group of eggs is ready to take their place, as can be seen in the upper body of the shrimp. A few days after the mature eggs hatch, the new eggs will be laid and gathered under the tail to mature. We have seen some female shrimp in continuous egg production year-round.

SNAIL: EPITONIUM BILLEANUM CORAL: FAMILY DENDROPHYLLIIDAE

NUDIBRANCH: UNDESCRIBED NEMBROTHA SP.

The long proboscis of the snail at left has found its way into the soft parts of an orange cup coral. The snail—and its eggs— blend in with the coral because of a dye that it receives from the flesh of the coral. When disturbed, these snails can release a toxic yellow substance, a defense mechanism that also comes courtesy of their prey.

Instead of struggling with the sea squirt's tough tunic, this clever nudibranch climbed on a bit of algae and attacked the sea squirt through its incurrent siphon. The nudibranch then began to scrape out the tender zooid inside, using the rasping structure seen protruding from its mouth in this photograph.

DAMSELFISH: CHRYSIPTERA CYANEA

The brilliant electric color of this fish taxes the ability of print-er's ink on a page to reproduce. The blue devil damselfish is not uncommon, and small groups, hovering around coral heads, can be found inside lagoons and in the shallow parts of the reef. The groups consist of one male, which has a bright yellow tail, and several females, like the one above.

This nudibranch has such a tough body that it looks and feels like a child's toy. It is a large—perhaps four inches long—and conspicuous animal, and moves excruciatingly slowly. If dis-turbed, *Notodoris* seizes into a rubbery mass and releases its hold of the bottom. It will not relax and reattach itself for quite some time.

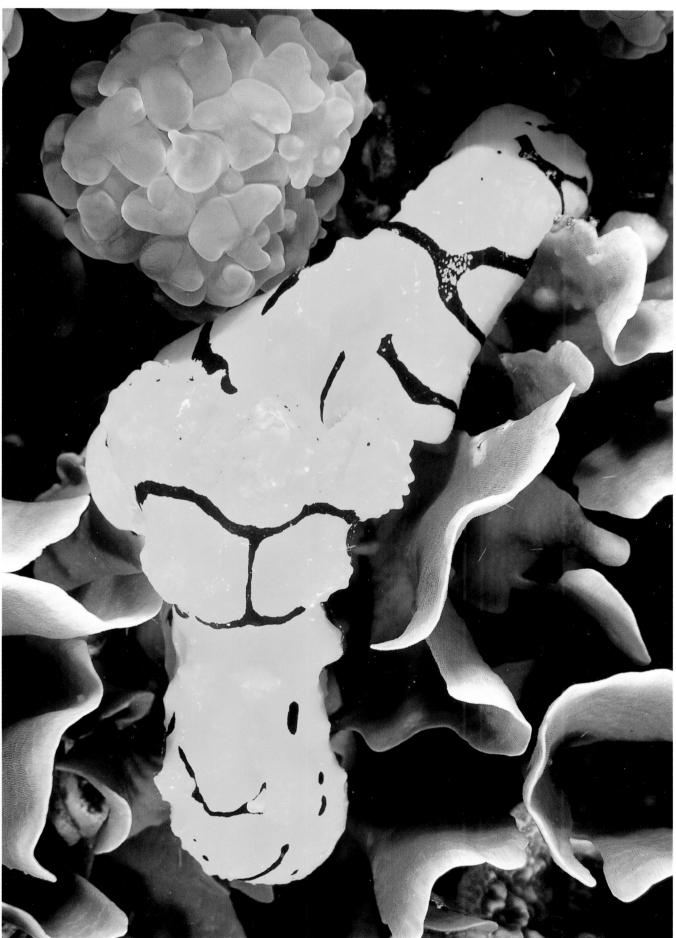

NUDIBRANCH:NOTODORIS MINOR

CUTTLEFISH: SEPIA SP.

SQUID: FAMILY SEPIOLIDAE

Female cuttlefish in the Lembeh Strait attach their eggs to the undersides of rock slabs, sometimes right up against the shoreline in just a few feet of water. As the embryonic cuttlefish mature, their movements become visible through the transparent egg cases. The moment of hatching, caught on film here, takes just a split second as, in a single motion, the cuttlefish pierces the egg case and jets away.

When I first encountered it on a night dive, this shy squid tried to hide by lying on the bottom and pulling sand over itself with its tentacles. When it saw I wasn't leaving, however, it abandoned this strategy and darted away. It wasn't until the transparencies were developed that I saw the strange position the squid had assumed during its escape. The speed is evident by the thin trail of ink but the raised tentacles seem as if they would hinder, rather than help, the getaway.

The anglerfish relies on camouflage and the element of surprise to catch its prey. It crouches motionless against the substrate, breathing quietly through its slightly open mouth and discretely expelling water through small openings behind its leg-like pectoral fins. It attracts curious fish to within range by manipulating a little lure above its mouth. The anglerfish's strike is one of the quickest movements in nature—only the mouth extends; its body remains still. The speed and subtlety of the strike are such that it is unlikely the schooling cardinalfish will even notice the sudden disappearance of their companion.

ANGLERFISH: ANTENNARIUS COMMERSONI

FALSE CATFISH: PHOLODICHTHYS LEUCOTAENIA CORAL: SINULARIA FLEXIBILIS

SWEETLIPS: PLECTORHINCHUS CHAETODONOIDES

Unlike gorgonians, which are stiffened with a horny material, the current tosses about the limp branches of this soft coral with ease. When young, these false catfish mimic the pattern, body shape and schooling behavior of juvenile striped eel catfish. False catfish do not possess the venomous spines of the true catfish, but the act is good enough that predators give them a wide berth.

While I watched, this juvenile many spotted sweetlips performed its erratic, twisting dance without pause. This odd behavior is thought to be the fish's way of mimicking a poisonous nudibranch or flatworm. Only the juvenile dances this way, and as it matures the fish also loses the strong pattern and flowing fins that make the act believable.

ANEMONES: NEMANTHUS SP.

The beautiful colonial anemones above are opportunistic colonizers of gorgonians, black corals and hydroids. In this case, they have fastened themselves to the dead skeleton of a whip coral, positioning themselves to feed in the current.

These strange shrimp blend so well with their host that they are hardly noticeable. It was only after I had watched them for some time, busily picking material from the surface of the black coral bush, that I realized just how many were there.

SHRIMP: TOZEUMA SP. BLACK CORAL: ANTIPATHES SP.

SQUID: SEPIOTEUTHIS LESSONIANA   WIRE CORAL: CIRRHIPATHES SPIRALIS

REMORA: ECHENEIS NAUCRATES

Only once in a great while do I come across a cooperative squid, and even then it usually absorbs the light from my strobes, producing dark photographs. This one lingered around the wire coral, and accommodated me by maintaining its light color while I took pictures. The squid's two long mating tentacles appear to be extended; although I didn't see another squid in the area, I may have interrupted an amorous moment.

The remora uses an unusual sucking-disk on top of its head to attach to larger animals, including manta rays, sharks, turtles and, on occasion, even divers. Attaching to a host does not assure the remora's protection, and aggressive jacks will attack them repeatedly even as they cling desperately to their host. The remora opens its mouth and strains plankton while riding, but if the host is predatory and bits of food become available while it is feeding, the remora will detach momentarily to snap up the scraps.

SEA STAR: FROMIA MONILIS

The bright red "button" on the top of this sea star is the madreporite, a kind of sieve that allows the starfish to manage its internal vascular system. This complex network of fluid-filled canals and hydraulically operated tube feet gives sea stars the mobility and subtle strength they need to locate and capture prey on the reef.

Chromodorid nudibranchs are among the most familiar to divers both because the family is the largest—with more than 300 named species—and because many of its members move about in the open during the day. They feed on sponges, and the toxins used by the sponges to keep from being overgrown with algae and encrusting animals are retained by the nudibranchs to make them unpalatable.

NUDIBRANCH: CHROMODORIS COI

ANGLERFISH: ANTENNARIUS COMMERSONI   TUNICATES: RHOPALAEA SP.

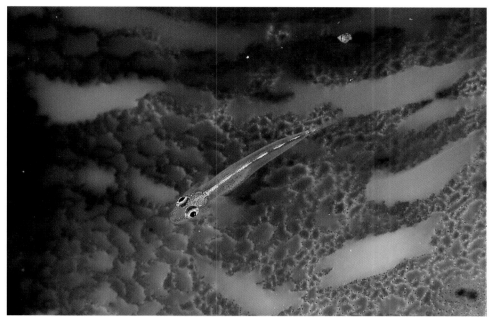

GOBY: PLEUROSICYA MOFFAMBICA   CLAM: TRIDACNA GIGAS

The young anglerfish at left has extended its fleshy lure, or esca, to attract prey. Although this specimen is just an inch-and-a-half long, it has a deceptively large mouth and could potentially eat another fish almost its own size. No fish approached while I watched, but several small swimming crustaceans passed by, and these were consumed in a series of lightning fast strikes.

This cling goby lives on the mantle of a giant clam, cleaning the surface of debris and parasites in exchange for the shelter of its fleshy folds. The dramatic pattern and coloration of the mantle of the giant clam is related to the presence in its tissues of a symbiotic alga that supplies much of the clam's nutritional needs. While photographing the goby, the clam suddenly closed on my camera housing. Reasoning the filter-feeding clam didn't really want to eat my camera, and hoping it wouldn't crush it by accident, I held on and pulled gently until I was able to extract it undamaged.

DEVILFISH: INIMICUS DIDACTYLUS

This hoary and bristled creature is the spiny devilfish. If its appearance is not enough to deter one from bothering it, its genus name—*Inimicus*—should make the point more clearly. This is one of the most venomous fish known. For all its reputation, *Inimicus* is actually a rather unassuming and very interesting animal. The first two rays of its pectoral fins have developed into mobile little claspers, with which it can walk across the gravel. When found over finer substrate, *Inimicus* will often bury itself up to its eyes, lying in wait for crustaceans and small fishes. As can be seen here, algae, bryozoans and other encrusting invertebrates will literally grow on this fish's skin, further aiding its camouflage. The bright red color of this individual is quite unusual.

A successful strike does not necessarily assure a meal. Having ambushed a small sharpnose puffer, this clearfin lizardfish now has a choice. It can hang on and wait until the puffer deflates and can be swallowed, or it can let go and make another attempt later. This one held on, but the pufferfish continued to look around almost casually for an opportunity that might allow its escape.

LIZARDFISH: SYNODUS DERMATOGENYS   PUFFER: CANTHIGASTER SP.

UNIDENTIFIED MANTIS SHRIMP

MANTIS SHRIMP: ODONTODACTYLUS SCYLLARIS

Mantis shrimp are members of an interesting order of crustaceans that possess highly modified and specialized feeding appendages. The mantis shrimp at left, poised at the entrance to its burrow, waits for soft-bodied prey to come within range, and then, in a split-second, seizes them in its spiny raptorial legs, in the same manner as its namesake. Instead of spines, the raptorial legs of the animal above terminate in stout knobs, which it uses to smash hard-bodied crustaceans. This species is a very active predator, leaving its burrow and searching the reef by day.

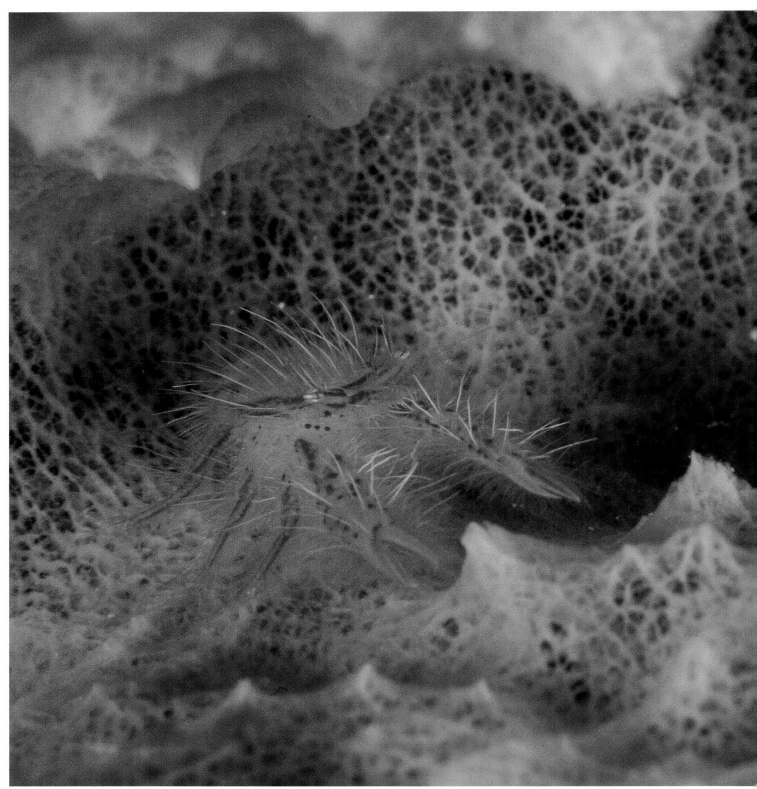

SQUAT LOBSTER: LAURIEA SIAGIANI

The deep folds on the outside of a barrel sponge provide excellent shelter for these commensal squat lobsters. Also, water is constantly flowing and being actively drawn through pores on the outer surface of the sponge, and plankton and particles too large for the sponge's needs collect there. For the squat lobsters, it is like living on the surface of a huge food screen. The fine hairs on their bodies alert them to their body position in relation to the sponge, and to sudden water movements that might indicate predators or prey.

UNIDENTIFIED CRAB CORAL: PLEROGYRA SINUOSA FLATWORMS: ORDER ACOELA

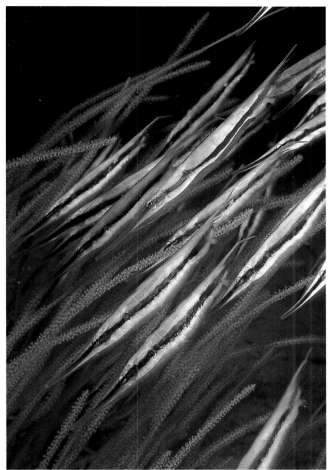

SHRIMPFISH: AEOLISCUS STRIGATUS   GORGONIAN: FAMILY ELLISELLIDAE

The furry body of this crab makes it look like a piece of debris that has become lodged among the balloon-like vesicles of this bubble coral. The odd vesicles contain stinging cells and are thought to serve a protective function. At night the "bubbles" collapse, and the coral extends thin tentacles to trap plankton. Flatworms roam the surface of the vesicles, living on organic matter sticking to them.

During the day these shrimpfish travel about the reef in small groups, but at night they gather together in a school among the branches of this pink gorgonian. One night we inadvertently flushed a large group from its hiding place, and the panicked little fish then gathered around our heads in the darkness, where we could feel them lightly touching our ears and hair.

CRAB: NEOPETROLISTHES SP.

Tucked in a crevice at night, the porcelain crab above feeds by smoothly sweeping its delicate mandibular sieves through the water. After several quick sweeps, the crab passes them through its mouth and removes the plankton that has been strained from the passing current. It then deploys its sieves once again.

The longnose hawkfish lives on deeper slopes and walls exposed to strong currents. It is almost always found in black coral bushes—as here—or in gorgonians, although I have seen specimens resting on the bottom among cup corals and snowflake corals. It feeds on small planktonic and benthic crustaceans.

HAWKFISH: OXYCIRRHITES TYPUS   BLACK CORAL: ANTIPATHES SP.

BARRACUDA: SPHYRAENA PUTNAMIAE

BARRACUDA: SPHYRAENA PUTNAMIAE

During the day, chevroned barracuda gather in midwater in large schools, which change shape as if they were a single, huge organism. At night the schools disperse, and individual fish roam the water column beyond the reef. When I first saw the barracuda they were stationary over the reef, being cleaned by a dozen pennant butterflyfish. At my approach they moved out into blue water, forming a ball which began slowly to rotate. The shape of the school evolved from a ball into a ring and then dissolved, only to reform once more further off.

CRAB: LISSOCARCINUS ORBICULARIS

In the photograph above, a commensal crab crawls into the mouth of its host sea cucumber like a living pill. The crab's coloration and low body profile render it practically invisible as it roams the surface of the sea cucumber, but when it feels in need of shelter it crawls over to the mouth, watching warily. If the situation mandates, the little crab pulls itself inside.

This pink anemonefish is momentarily agitated as its host has decided to contract, becoming a smooth sphere and giving the fish nowhere to hide. Although in maximum diameter it is slightly exceeded by the short-napped Merten's anemone, in overall mass the magnificent anemone is the largest anemone in the world. It also tends to prefer shallow, exposed locations where it is quite easy for divers to spot.

ANEMONEFISH: AMPHIPRION PERIDERAION   SEA ANEMONE: HETERACTIS MAGNIFICA

SNAKE EEL: FAMILY OPHICHTHIDAE

Because of their habit of burying themselves in the sand, snake eels are not often noticed by divers. They are also not often noticed by passing fish, which is the reason for this secretive behavior. They have strong jaws and sharp teeth, and are very capable predators. Some species leave the sand occasionally to forage, particularly at night.

This red-spotted blenny has tucked itself into a hole for protection. When the coast is clear, it will venture out onto the reef to graze on algae, and the small organisms living on it. The blenny's downturned mouth contains hundreds of tiny teeth with which it scrapes the algae from the rocks.

BLENNY: ISTIBLENNIUS CHRYSOSPILOS

OCTOPUS: HAPALOCHLAENA LUNULATA

OCTOPUS: HAPALOCHLAENA LUNULATA

When not excited, the coloration of the blue-ringed octopus is so cryptic that it is simply invisible. Although I had spent days looking for just this species, it was almost an accident that I got these photos. Kneeling in six feet of water, I was watching a decorator crab when—suddenly—those brilliant blue flashing rings. The octopus must have accepted my presence in his territory, as he had killed a crab right under my nose. The excitement of the initial attack brought out the brightest blue color from the rings, and they faded to green before the animal tucked the crab in its skirt and crept calmly away. Blue-ringed octopus are small, and like most octopi, short-lived. Despite their modest size, their bite is very dangerous.

OCTOPUS: HAPALOCHLAENA LUNULATA

CRAB: FAMILY PORCELLANIDAE   CORAL: DENDRONEPHTHYA SP.

Coloration that matches the beautiful *Dendronephthya* soft coral offers this porcelain crab some protection. The crab feeds during the day using specialized feeding sieves to strain the water for plankton. This one was very nervous, and on my approach hid for a few minutes before resuming feeding.

Brandishing a piece of a brittle starfish in its claw and sprouting head ornaments consisting of sprigs of stinging hydroid, this spider crab means to be considered a tough customer. The transplanted defenses and its pugilistic tendencies serve to protect the small crab as it forages in the shallow waters of the reef at night.

UNIDENTIFIED CRAB

The silvery crown on this featherduster worm is actually a highly sophisticated "sieve" to capture plankton and other particles from the water. Material sticking to the feathery pinnules is carried by beating cilia to a groove in the stem of the radiole—the "quill" of each "feather"—and from there to the worm's mouth. The V-shaped groove also acts as a size sorting mechanism: particles too large to fit the groove are washed off by the current, medium-sized particles that sit high in the groove are segregated and used in tube-building, and the tiniest particles, which sit deep in the groove, are ingested.

WORM: SABELLASTARTE SANCTIJOSEPHI   CORAL: EUPHYLLIA ANCORA

COWFISH: LACTORIA FORNASINI

As if its bony carapace were not a great enough deterrent to predators, the thornback cowfish sports no less than five tough-looking horns. With these defenses it probably doesn't matter that the fish is a clumsy swimmer.

This shrimp's unusual posture has a defensive purpose. By folding its pincers together, its head mimics its tail, which confuses predators—they can't quite tell at which end to strike. If they strike anyway, the shrimp has a 50 percent chance that they aimed for the wrong end, in which case it can escape or survive with just mild injuries. For additional protection, the shrimp stays near the stinging tentacles of a cerianthid, or tube anemone.

SHRIMP: PERICLIMENES SP.   UNIDENTIFIED CERIANTHID

SHRIMPFISH: AEOLISCUS STRIGATUS

DARTFISH: NEMATELEOTRIS MAGNIFICA

Shrimpfish, at left, are uniquely constructed for horizontal travel while in a constant vertical position. In the course of evolution, their dorsal fin, tail and anal fins have all migrated to the same side of their bodies. During the day, shrimpfish travel across the reef flat, always head-down, in search of small crustaceans. At night the groups bunch together for safety among the branches of gorgonians.

These fire dartfish are plucking plankton from a current-swept area of the reef. They are nervous fish, and hover daintily over the bottom, continually flicking their long dorsal spines. At the first hint of danger they dive into the sand.

OVULID: PSEUDOSIMNIA INCISA   CORAL: DENDRONEPHTHYA SP.

Like cowries, for which they are sometimes mistaken, ovulids have a mantle that can completely cover their shells. When the mantle of this ovulid is fully extended, it is just about impossible to see it on its host soft coral. The ovulid is a parasite: through its entire life, it will use the coral for food, shelter and a place to lay its eggs.

This commensal shrimp perches on the very tip of a sea anemone tentacle and swivels its body to attract fish for its cleaning services. Since the fish would be stung if they touched the anemone's tentacles, the shrimp has to jump up onto its clients to clean them.

SHRIMP: PERICLIMENES HOLTHUISI   SEA ANEMONE: HETERACTIS MAGNIFICA

CRAB: HOPLOPHYRS OATESII   CORAL: DENDRONEPHTHYA SP.

SHRIMP: STENOPUS TENUIROSTRIS

What alerted me to this crab's presence on the soft coral branch was a clump of the soft coral pulled tightly over her body. This female crab is in berry, and hides herself and her abdomen full of eggs during the day. Only at night does she emerge to feed among the branches of the coral.

The red and white bands on this cleaner shrimp, like a barber's pole, help advertise its grooming services. While the large, banded claws may attract fish, it is the two pairs of tiny claws beneath them that do the actual cleaning.

WORM: PROTULA MAGNIFICA

The graceful feeding structures of this polychaete worm are attached to a soft, segmented body hidden in a dark tube. The worm's body is modified for such an existence, and special beating cilia keep water circulating inside the tube. Since its soft body is protected, only the spiralled food-gathering filaments are risked when feeding, and these can quickly be regenerated if lost to a hungry wrasse.

Blanketed with sea anemone—like corallimorpharians, and wearing a tunicate on its knee, this decorator crab looks a bit overdressed. At least it left room for its eyes. When the crab molts, it will have to transfer its living clothing to its new shell, or perhaps leave them and acquire new ones.

CRAB: MICIPPA PHILYRA   CORALLIMORPHARIANS: DISCOSOMA SP.   TUNICATE: DIADEMNUM SP.

PUFFER: AROTHRON NIGROPUNCTATUS

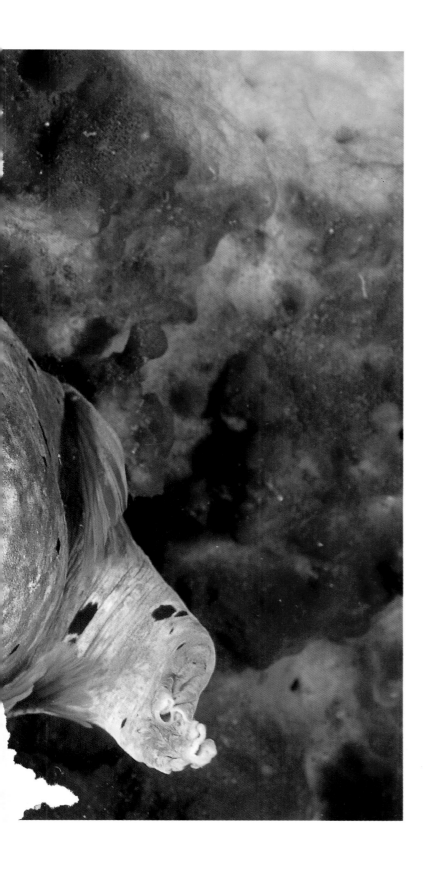

Having apparently done enough work for the day, this black-spotted puffer has stuffed its pliant body into the crook of a sponge. This easily approached species has mobile, animated eyes and the gentle countenance of a dog. When swimming, puffers appear almost clumsy, but because of their ability to inflate, and the fact that their skin and viscera contain tetraodontoxin, one of the most powerful toxins known, they face little danger of being eaten.

EEL: BRACHYSOMOPHIS HENSHAWI

With dead-looking, reptilian eyes and a disposition to match, the Henshaw eel lurks buried in the sand, waiting for a fish to pass by. When one does, the eel seizes it in its powerful jaws and drags the victim underneath the sand to be eaten. The Henshaw eel's jaws are larger than can be seen in this photo, and it will take a surprisingly large fish.

The commensal porcelain crab lives in the stinging carpet of a sea anemone. It feeds by sifting plankton from the water, but while doing so remains securely anchored to the anemone. When not feeding, the crab slips beneath the anemone's skirt to hide.

CRAB: NEOPETROLISTHES OHSHIMAI   SEA ANEMONE: STICHODACTYLA SP.

147

SNAPPER: MACOLOR MACULARIS   FAIRY BASSLETS: PSEUDANTHIAS DISPAR, PSEUDANTHIAS SQUAMMIPINNIS

NUDIBRANCH: UNDESCRIBED HALGERDA SP.

Frequent strong currents past this point off Bunaken Island supply food to a colorful assemblage of plankton feeders. Current-swept points are good places to see large, mixed schools of fairy basslets and damsels. The young snapper in the center still shows signs of its juvenile pattern, although it is beginning to fade.

The orange net pattern on its body, and the brown speckling on its gills and rhinophores serve to break up the outline of this nudibranch, making it less visible. Even if the animal were noticed, however, noxious chemicals concentrated in the orange dots in the mantle would discourage most predators from eating it.

GOBY: AMBLYELEOTRIS SP.   SHRIMP: ALPHEUS RANDALLI

This flagtail shrimp goby and its symbiotic companion shrimp are a frequently seen combination around North Sulawesi. The fish warns the nearly blind shrimp of danger through its body movements, a signal the shrimp receives through its antenna, which is always laid against the fish. I have seen somewhat slow-witted shrimps ignore their partner's repeated warnings, and in these cases the agitated fish literally bullies the shrimp back down into the burrow.

These crabs, like synchronized dancers, have assumed identical positions to feed among the limbs of their host sea pen. Each holds up the frond of the sea pen with one claw while deploying its feeding fan. The other claw is folded carefully out of the way, so as not to block the plankton-rich current.

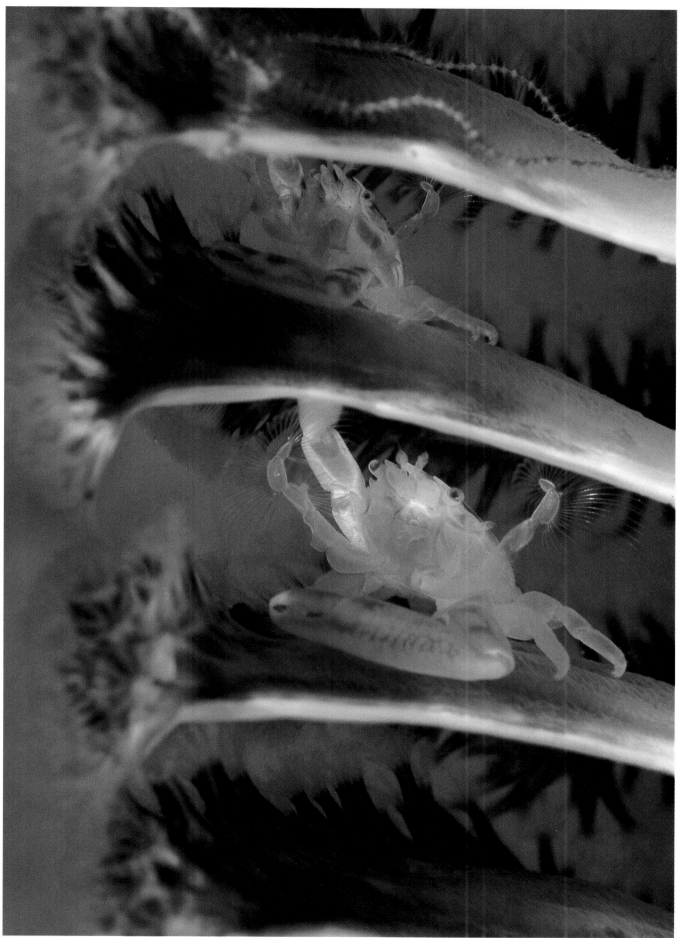

CRAB: FAMILY PORCELLANIDAE   SEA PEN: PTEROEIDES SP.

OCTOPUS: OCTOPUS SP.

OCTOPUS: OCTOPUS SP.

The small, unidentified species of octopus at left had partially burrowed into the coarse sandy bottom. This animal, found in the Lembeh area, is one of the many poorly understood octopus species that can be found on Sulawesi's reefs. Reef octopus have keen eyesight and are formidable predators of crabs, which they subdue with their strong arms and venomous bite.

Above is another unidentified octopus from Lembeh, but this one was confident and showed little fear of my presence. Octopus are generally quite shy, and small, brightly-colored species that don't run away make me think that they are probably armed with powerful venom. This may be the first record of this species.

BLENNY: ECSENIUS BICOLOR   CORAL: PECTINIA LACTUCA

Bicolor blennies like the one pictured above can often be seen resting on the coral formations along the walls of Bunaken Island. Every now and then they leave their perches to
swim out after small planktonic animals. This species is unusually nonchalant for such a
small fish, and it has been suggested that this is because of its close resemblance to the
venomous yellowtail fangblenny.

The yellowskin goby lives exclusively in the maze of branches produced by the delicate
needle coral, which is common in shallow, protected waters. Because of the fine coral
branches, I found it very difficult to get a clear shot of the goby and this photograph was
deceptively hard to take. Not until I saw the developed transparency did I notice the fine
papillae—like a beard—on this tiny fish.

GOBY: PARAGOBIODON XANTHOSOMUS   CORAL: SERIATOPORA HYSTRIX

BANNERFISH: HENIOCHUS ACUMINATUS   EMPEROR: LUTJANUS SEBAE   SEA URCHIN: ASTROPYGA RADIATA

CORAL: EUPHYLLIA ANCORA

The urchin at left became a mobile home when a crab rose from beneath the sand, clamped its rear legs around the urchin, and carried it off as a form of protection. When I approached, the crab let go and buried itself into the silt. The urchin provided the only shelter within hundreds of feet, and a cluster of juvenile pennant bannerfish hovered above its spines. The flash of black and white between the urchin's spines is a juvenile red emperor, which had been trying fruitlessly to convince the crab to change directions and carry the urchin away from me.

The large, dramatic tentacles of corals of the genus *Euphyllia* make them among the most beautiful of their kind. The species pictured above shares the distinction with another *Euphyllia* of being one of only two species of corals that even experts cannot distinguished by their skeletons. The living polyps of the two are so distinct, however, that even a beginner will notice the difference.

ACKNOWLEDGEMENTS

The authors would like to thank those whose generosity and interest made the photographs in this book possible long before we even knew they would be in this book. Our good friend, Loky Herlambang, provided boats, crews and lodging during frequent month-long stays at the Nusantara Diving Centre over the past seven years. Garuda Indonesia's Kathleen Heasley supported us by providing our tickets and continually pushing me to improve my photography. Mohammed Hasir, Garuda's Ujung Pandang station manager, became a safe haven for our nightmarishly overweight equipment. And John Paul of Aqua Vision Systems managed to keep me going with his remarkable generosity and exceptionally rugged underwater housings and equipment.

Many others were of particular help. The late Dr. Noboru Fukui opened our eyes to the varieties of diving in North Sulawesi and is sorely missed. Our friend, Kal Muller, Bahasa speaker and Indonesia traveler, introduced us to Kungkungan Bay Resort and opened our eyes to all of Indonesia which he loves so well. Kungkungan Bay's Dorothy and Mark Ecenbarger showed us the Straits of Lembeh in magnificent style, and have a keen desire to understand the marine environment of the Lembeh area they are so dedicated to preserving. Their support has been unflagging during this project.

Also crucial to this book were the experts who tackled the formidable task of marine life identifications: Dr. John E. Randall, Senior Ichthyologist at the Bernice Pauahi Bishop Museum in Honolulu, identified our fish; Dr. Terrence M. Gosliner and Dr. Gary Williams, both of the California Academy of Sciences in San Francisco, helped identify the invertebrates, especially the nudibranchs and soft corals; Dr. Mary Wicksten of Texas A&M University identified many of the crustaceans; and Dr. Clyde Roper, National Museum of Natural History, Smithsonian Institution, gave us names for our baffling octopus and squid.

And of course we would like to thank the captains, crews and guides who got us to the sites, helped find animals, and got us back home safely, time and again: Reinhart Garang, whose sense of humor and generosity gave us a much deeper appreciation for the warmth and kindness of our Indonesian hosts; Saleh Lahengko, boatman extraordinaire, who can make anything burn if it means lighting his cigarette; Maya Makalew, diver and model; Dolphi Nicolas, camera assistant and captain; Daeing Samsudin, the best animal finder of all; and Engel Lamakeki, friend, Bahasa instructor and boat captain, who has followed my bubble trail through the pouring rain for hours on end.

The most difficult person to thank is our good friend David Pickell. Without his fine sense of composition and design, editorial persistence, and dedication, this book would never have come about.

INDEX